An introduction to the
BUTTERFLIES OF CYPRUS

A photographic pocket guide
to the identification of the
resident species and regular immigrants

Adrian M. Riley

Brambleby Books

An introduction to the butterflies of Cyprus

Text © Adrian M Riley 2024

All the photos were taken by the author unless otherwise stated.

The author has asserted his rights under the Copyright, Designs and Patents Act 1988 to be identified as the Author of this Work. All Rights Reserved.

No part of this book may be reproduced in any form by photocopying or by any electronic or mechanical means, including information, storage or retrieval systems, without permission in writing from both the copyright owners and the publisher of this book.

ISBN 9781908241764

Published 2024 by
Brambleby Books, Devon, UK

www.bramblebybooks.co.uk

Book layout by Tanya Warren, Creatix Design

Printed and bound by
Short Run Press Ltd., Devon, UK

To my friends
Brian and Celia Greatwood

Oh! You Pretty Things
David Bowie (1947-2016)

Beautifully camouflaged Mallow Skipper

Spring female Fiery Copper

About the Author

Adrian Riley grew up in Shropshire where his deep interest and knowledge about wildlife, especially butterflies, moths and birds, first took root. For over forty years he has worked as a professional entomologist and moth recorder for the world-famous Rothamsted agricultural research station in Harpenden, Hertfordshire. For the past twenty years he has lived in Norfolk from where he has led wildlife tours, both in the UK and mainland Europe.

Adrian is the author of numerous books about wildlife, including field guides such as *British and Irish Butterflies, Dragons and Damsels* and *Norfolk Wildlife*, and his anthropological account *Arrivals and Rivals: duel for the winning bird* (all four published by Brambleby Books), the latter concerning his aim to see as many bird species as possible throughout the British Isles within a single year.

Dew-covered Dark Grass Blue in the dawn light

Mating pair of Paphos Blue butterflies

Contents

Introduction 10

Acknowledgements 12

Taxonomic list of species 13

BUTTERFLY GROUPS

Swallowtails and Festoons 18
Skippers 24
Yellows 32
Whites 35
Coppers 45
Leopards 48
Blues and Hairstreaks 50
Vanessids and Fritillaries 72
Snouts 78
Pashas and Tigers 79
Browns 82

Index of species 100

Checklist 104

Introduction

Cyprus is not only a popular holiday destination but is also visited by birdwatchers in their hundreds during the Spring and Autumn avian migrations. Many of these travel from the UK. Most have at least a passing interest in other wildlife, and the majority are keen butterfly-watchers and photographers. I often receive images of butterflies with a request for help in their identification.

At the time of writing, there are four books dealing with Cyprus butterflies:
1. Makris, C. (2003) *Butterflies of Cyprus*. Bank of Cyprus Cultural Foundation.
2. Sparrow, D. J. & John, E. (eds) (2016) *An Introduction to the Wildlife of Cyprus* (Chapter 15). Terra Cypria.
3. John, E. & Makris, C. (2022) *Butterflies of Cyprus: A Field Guide and Distribution Atlas*. CABI.
4. John, E. & Makris, C. (2023) *A Field Guide to the Butterflies of Cyprus with Distribution Maps.* Siri Scientific Press.

The text of the first book dealing with distribution and abundance is now out of date and has been superseded by John & Makris' 2022 & 2023 publications. The second is a mighty tome dealing with all of Cyprus's wildlife with only a single chapter, though very detailed, on butterflies. The third is an excellent account of the butterflies and contains a great deal of information that is of immense value to serious students of the subject that will probably never be surpassed. However, it may be a little overwhelming to the general naturalist with only a passing interest in butterflies. At 1.2 kg, its physical weight must also be taken into consideration, as must its expensive retail price. Thankfully, to help identify these insects there is now the website www.cyprusbutterflies.co.uk, which was created by the author's highly respected friend and colleague Dr Eddie John. However, access to the internet may not be available whilst working in the field, whereas a small identification guide, such as the present work, can be referred to anywhere and at any time. The fourth book, an abridged version of the third, attempts to address this problem but fails to do so with the lack of several important illustrations. The most serious of these is the omission of upperside photographs of the Holly Blue and female uppersides of the Little Tiger Blue, Paphos Blue, Persian (Small) Desert Blue, Dark (African) Grass Blue and Speckled Wood, and the male upperside of the Purple Hairstreak. These are omissions likely to prevent correct identification of these species.

The country has a total of 49 species of butterfly, of which three are endemic species (Paphos Blue, Cyprus Grayling and Cyprus Meadow Brown), five are endemic subspecies (Eastern Festoon, Levantine Leopard, The Hermit, Eastern Rock Grayling and Oriental Meadow Brown) and one regular visitor (Plain Tiger) which has bred here on at least one occasion, perhaps most notably in 2023. One of the species, the Nettle-tree Butterfly, is now protected by law and, of course, should thus not be disturbed in any way. The Lime Swallowtail arrived in the island in the autumn of 2021 and has since spread considerably as a breeding species. It is now a common sight around the suburbs of Nicosia.

It is not the purpose of this book to inform readers where to find the various species but rather how to identify those when found in the field. Distribution maps are given by John & Makris (2022, 2023) and are useful guides for anyone wishing to find a particular species. It is not an account of the biology of the insects. This is dealt with expertly by the aforementioned authors, though details of flight periods, foodplants, habitats and general distribution are given here as aids to identification.

A further important reason for writing this book is to encourage visitors to submit their records. This can easily be done by email to the Cyprus Butterfly Study Group (CBSG2012@gmail.com).

In light of these factors, I therefore hope that this volume will, for the first time in a book of its type, provide all of the necessary images and text needed to identify any of the island's resident butterflies and regular visitors. Also, I hope it encourages the formal submission of records and therefore improve our knowledge of the wildlife of this fascinating and beautiful island.

Adrian M. Riley.

Acknowledgements

The author is greatly indebted to the help given by Dr Eddie John and Dr Yiannis Christofides. Without their help much time would have been wasted in search of many of the photographs contained herein. I am also indebted to Christodoulos Makris for the information I gleaned during my early visits to the island from his wonderful book *Butterflies of Cyprus* (*Loc. cit.*). Without his work I would have been lost for a starting point for my studies. Matt Smith and Dave and Ros. Sparrow have been very helpful in suggesting sites to visit for specific species.

I also thank my friends Brian and Celia Greatwood of Agios Georgios, Pegia, for their generous hospitality and kindness during my many visits to the island. The days in the field were fun in their company and the evenings were filled with witty banter and delicious Cypriot food. I am also grateful to Matt Rowlings, Pieter Vantieghem, David Cook, Gary Thoburn, Steve Cale, Eddie John, Jason Moss, Dave & Ros. Sparrow, Geoffrey Pring, and Richard Harrington for generously providing photographs. Last but not least I thank Brambleby Books Ltd., and more specially Nicola Loxdale, for publishing this work and for her sterling editorial efforts.

Taxonomic List of residents and regular immigrants

The nomenclature and order of species follow that of Wiemers, M. *et al.* (2018) An updated checklist of the European Butterflies (Lepidoptera, Papilionoidea). *ZooKeys* **811**: 9-45.

* = Endemic subspecies
** = Endemic species

FAMILY: PAPILIONIDAE
1. Swallowtail *Papilio machaon* Linnaeus, 1758 subspecies *syriacus* Verity, 1905
2. Lime Swallowtail *Papilio demoleus* Linnaeus, 1758
3. Eastern Festoon *Zerynthia cerisyi* (Godart, 1824) subspecies *cypria* (Stichel, 1907) *

FAMILY: HESPERIIDAE
Subfamily HESPERIINAE
4. Millet Skipper *Pelopidas thrax* (Hübner, 1821)
5. Pigmy Skipper *Gegenes pumilio* (Hoffmannsegg, 1804)
6. Lulworth Skipper *Thymelicus acteon* (Rottemburg, 1775)

FAMILY: HESPERIIDAE Subfamily PYRGINAE
7. Mallow Skipper *Carcharodus alceae* (Esper, 1780)

FAMILY: PIERIDAE
8. Cleopatra *Gonepteryx cleopatra* (Linnaeus, 1767) subspecies *taurica* (Staudinger, 1881)
9. Clouded Yellow *Colias croceus* (Geoffroy, 1758)
10. Black-veined White *Aporia crataegi* (Linnaeus, 1758)
11. Bath White *Pontia daplidice* (Linnaeus, 1758)
12. Small Bath White *Pontia chloridice* (Hübner, [1813])
13. Large White *Pieris brassicae* (Linnaeus, 1758)
14. Small White *Pieris rapae* (Linnaeus, 1758)

15. Eastern Dappled White *Euchloe ausonia* (Hübner, 1804)
16. Orange-tip *Anthocharis cardamines* (Linnaeus, 1758)

FAMILY: LYCAENIDAE Subfamily LYCAENINAE
17. Small Copper *Lycaena phlaeas* (Linnaeus, 1761)
18. Lesser Fiery Copper *Lycaena thersamon* (Esper, 1764)

FAMILY: LYCAENIDAE Subfamily APHNAEINAE
19. Levantine Leopard *Apharitis acamas* (Klug, 1834) subspecies *cypriaca* Riley, 1925 *

FAMILY: LYCAENIDAE Subfamily THECLINAE
20. Purple Hairstreak *Favonius quercus* (Linnaeus, 1758)

FAMILY: LYCAENIDAE Subfamily POLYOMMATINAE
21. Lang's Short-tailed Blue *Leptotes pirithous* (Linnaeus, 1767)
22. Long-tailed Blue *Lampides boeticus* (Linnaeus, 1767)
23. Holly Blue *Celastrina argiolus* (Linnaeus, 1758)
24. Little Tiger Blue *Tarucus balkanicus* (Linnaeus, 1767)
25. Eastern Baton Blue *Pseudophilotes vicrama* (Moore, 1865)
26. Paphos Blue *Glaucopsyche paphos* Chapman, 1920 **
27. Dark (African) Grass Blue *Zizeeria karsandra* (Moore, 1865)
28. Persian (Small) Desert Blue *Luthrodes galba* (Lederer, 1855)
29. Grass Jewel *Freyeria trochylus* (Freyer, 1844)
30. Brown Argus *Aricia agestis* ([Denis & Schiffermüller, 1775])
31. Common Blue *Polyommatus icarus* (Rottemburg, 1775)

FAMILY: NYMPHALIDAE Subfamily LIMENITIDINAE
32. Southern White Admiral *Limenitis reducta* (Staudinger, 1901)

FAMILY: NYMPHALIDAE Subfamily HELICONIINAE
33. Cardinal *Argynnis pandora* ([Denis & Schiffermüller])

FAMILY: NYMPHALIDAE Subfamily NYMPHALINAE
34. Red Admiral *Vanessa atalanta* (Linnaeus, 1758)
35. Painted Lady *Vanessa cardui* (Linnaeus, 1758)

FAMILY: NYMPHALIDAE Subfamily LIBYTHEINAE
36. Nettle-tree Butterfly *Libythea celtis* ([Laicharting, 1782])

FAMILY: NYMPHALIDAE Subfamily DANAINAE
37. Plain Tiger *Danaus chrysippus* (Linnaeus, 1758)

FAMILY: NYMPHALIDAE Subfamily CHARAXINAE
38. Two-tailed Pasha *Charaxes jasius* (Linnaeus, 1767)

FAMILY: NYMPHALIDAE Subfamily SATYRINAE
39. Lattice Brown *Kirinia roxelana* (Cramer, 1777)
40. Speckled Wood *Pararge aegeria* (Linnaeus, 1758)
41. Large Wall Brown *Lasiommata maera* (Linnaeus, 1758)
42. Wall Brown *Lasiommata megera* (Linnaeus, 1767)
43. Eastern Rock Grayling *Hipparchia syriaca* (Staudinger, 1871) subspecies *cypriaca* (Staudinger, 1879) *
44. Cyprus Grayling *Hipparchia cypriensis* (Holik, 1949) **

45. The Hermit *Chazara briseis* (Linnaeus, 1764) subspecies *larnacarna* (Oberthür, 1909) *
46. White-banded Grayling *Pseudochazara anthelea* (Hübner, 1824)
47. African Ringlet *Ypthima asterope* (Klug, 1832)
48. Cyprus Meadow Brown *Maniola cypricola* (Graves, 1928) **
49. Oriental Meadow Brown *Hyponephele lupina* (Costa, 1836) subspecies *cypriaca* Riley, 1921 *

SCARCE VAGRANTS; EXTINCT RESIDENTS

African Migrant *Catopsilia florella* (Fabricius, 1775). Very scarce vagrant.

Brown-veined (Caper) White *Belenois aurota* (Fabricius, 1793). One record only.

Pomegranate Hairstreak *Deudorix livia* (Klug, 1834). One record only.

African Babul Blue *Azanus jesous* (Guèrin, 1849). A single recent record.

Large Tortoiseshell *Nymphalis polychloros* (Linnaeus, 1758). Extinct resident.

Queen of Spain Fritillary *Issoria lathonia* (Linnaeus, 1758). Three recent records.

False Plain Tiger *Hypolimnus misippus* (Linnaeus, 1764). Two records only.

Great Steppe Grayling *Chazara persephone* ([Hübner, 1805]). A single recent record.

Butterfly Groups, with page numbers

Swallowtails and Festoons 18

Skippers 24

Yellows 32

Whites 35

Coppers 45

Leopards 48

Blues and Hairstreaks 50

Vanessids and Fritillaries 72

Snouts 78

Pashas and Tigers 79

Browns 82

SPECIES ACCOUNTS

SWALLOWTAIL
Papilio machaon Linn.
subspecies *syriacus* Verity

Swallowtail

Distribution and habitat
Widely distributed and common in a variety of habitats wherever the larval hostplants grow. These include field edges, rough ground, flowery meadows and the edges of agricultural plots from sea level to the high mountains.

Foodplants
Usually Fennel *Foeniculum vulgare*, but other umbelliferous plants are also used.

Flight period
Usually from February to late October in three or more overlapping generations.

Identification

Average wingspan 70mm. As the only 'tailed' swallowtail found in Cyprus, this species is unmistakeable.

The distinctive 'feathery' foliage of Fennel

Coastal habitat near Kato Paphos

LIME SWALLOWTAIL
Papilio demoleus **Linn.**

Lime Swallowtail underside

Distribution and habitat
The Lime Swallowtail was first recorded in Cyprus during the autumn of 2021. Individuals overwintered successfully and produced spring progeny in 2022. From the points of origin in the east, it has spread during 2022 and 2023 into many areas where its foodplants are cultivated or grown in gardens. The species is well known for the ability to occupy new territory and maintain populations therein. It has gained pest status on cultivated citrus fruits in several countries bordering the eastern Mediterranean. In 2022, it was the most common butterfly on the wing during late September in the suburbs of Nicosia.

Lime Swallowtail upperside

Foodplants
Cultivated citrus fruits, including Lime, Lemon and Orange, though the first is uncommon in Cyprus.

Flight period
Seemingly multivoltine between, and including, April and November.

Identification
Very large with a wingspan of up to 100mm. It is unlike any other species in this region.

EASTERN FESTOON
Zerynthia cerisyi (Godart)
subspecies *cypria* (Stichel)

Distribution and habitat

This endemic subspecies is widely distributed and common in the south-western half of the island and may be encountered most frequently in upland areas where the hostplant grows near water. It is usually seen in scrubland, forests, agricultural land, roadside verges and dry riverbeds.

Eastern Festoon underside

Eastern Festoon upperside

Suitable flowery trackside habitat near Theletra

Foodplant
Birthwort *Aristolochia sempervirens*.
Flight period
Usually early March to early May in a single generation.
Identification
Average wingspan 60mm. The ground colour of the female is creamier than that of the male and the outer margins of the hindwings bear small red spots. As the only Festoon butterfly found in Cyprus, this species is unmistakeable.

The distinctive leaf shape of the foodplant

MILLET SKIPPER
Pelopidas thrax Hübner

Millet Skipper

Millet Skipper underside

Distribution and habitat
Widespread and locally common in lowland areas. It inhabits reedbeds, field edges, roadsides, abandoned plots and dry riverbeds where the foodplants occur. The number of individuals on the wing increases as the year progresses.

Foodplant
Mainly Common Reed (*Phragmites australis*), Smilograss (*Piptatherum milliaceum*) and probably other 'fine' grasses (Poaceae).

Flight period
Usually from early April to mid-Novermber in at least two generations.

Identification
Average wingspan 40mm. Similar to Pigmy Skipper. See text p26 for that species and Fig 1 p26. Pay particular attention to the shape of the end of the antennae.

Typical dry riverbed habitat

PIGMY SKIPPER
Gegenes pumilio (Hoffmannsegg)

Distribution and habitat
Found throughout Cyprus, most frequently in dry lowland areas, but never common. It frequents scrubland, abandoned plots, roadside verges and dry riverbeds.

Foodplant
Various 'fine' grasses (Poaceae).

Flight period
Usually early April to late November in at least three generations. The number of individuals on the wing increases as the year progresses.

Identification
Average wingspan 30mm. Easily confused with Millet Skipper from which it differs in the following ways (Fig 1):
1. Smaller with forewings shorter and less pointed.
2. Male upperside completely black.
3. Female upperside lacking two pale spots near the costa.

Pigmy Skipper female

Pigmy Skipper male

4. Underside of hindwing with pale patches rather than plain, with at least one bright white spot.
5. Tips of antennae blunt rather than hooked.
See Fig 1.

Fig 1. Distinguishing features of Pigmy and Millet Skipper

Pigmy Skipper | Millet Skipper

LULWORTH SKIPPER
Thymelicus acteon (Rottemburg)

Lulworth Skipper female

Lulworth Skipper male

Distribution and habitat
Widespread and common throughout Cyprus and found in many habitat types.
Foodplant
Various grasses
Flight period
Usually late April to early July.
Identification
Average wingspan 25mm. This is the only orange skipper butterfly found in Cyprus.

Clifftop grassland habitat near coastal Mandria

MALLOW SKIPPER
Carcharodus alceae (Esper)

Mallow Skipper upperside

Mallow Skipper underside

Distribution and habitat
A common and widespread species that occurs in many habitat types, particularly rough open ground.
Foodplant
Several species of mallow (Malvaceae), most often Common Mallow (*Malva sylvestris*).
Flight period
Usually from early February to mid-November in several generations.
Identification
Average wingspan 28mm. The beautifully marbled patterns on the uppersides make this species easy to identify.

Common Mallow

CLEOPATRA *Gonepteryx cleopatra* (Linn.) suspecies *taurica* (Staudinger)

Cleopatra female

Cleopatra male

Distribution and habitat
Widespread and common, though less so at lower elevations. It inhabits scrubland, forests and the margins of agricultural plots.
Foodplant
Mainly Mediterranean Buckthorn (*Rhamnus alaternus*).
Flight period
From February to mid-November in one, or possibly two, generations. The adults hibernate over the winter.
Identification
Average wingspan 58mm. The pointed apices to all the wings preclude confusion with other species. The Cleopatra always rests with its wings closed. In the male, the ground colour is more yellow than that of the female (illustrated). In flight, the large, bright orange patches on the male's forewings can be very striking.

Cleopatra habitat near Akrotiri

CLOUDED YELLOW
Colias croceus (Geoffroy)

Distribution and habitat
A very common species found in all habitat types throughout the island.

Foodplant
Several species of the pea family (Fabacea).

Flight period
Usually from mid-February to late November in several overlapping generations.

Identification
Average wingspan 47mm. Unmistakeable. Note: there is an uncommon form of the female in which the usual yellow colouration is replaced by white (below, right). This is known as form *helice* (Hübner, 1879).

Clouded Yellow typical male

Clouded Yellow female form *helice*

BLACK-VEINED WHITE
Aporia crataegi (Linn.)

Distribution and habitat
This is a localised species that is restricted to the Troodos highlands where it inhabits forests, scrubland and the edges of cultivated plots.

Foodplant
The hawthorn species Mediterranean Medlar (*Crataegus azarolus*).

Flight period
Usually mid-April to mid-June in a single generation.

Identification
Average wingspan 55mm. This large, white butterfly with conspicuous black 'veins' on the wings is unlike any other species found in Cyprus.

Black-veined White (Switzerland). Richard Harrington

Typical upland habitat near Mandria

BATH WHITE
Pontia daplidice (Linn.)

Distribution and habitat
A very common and widely distributed species that is found in most habitat types.

Foodplant
Many species of Resedaceae and Brassicaceae, including Wild Mignonette (*Resida lutea*) and various mustards (Cruciferae).

Flight period
Usually from early February to mid-November in several generations.

Identification.
Average wingspan 40mm. The uppersides of the male hindwings lack the dark markings of the female (figured). This species may be confused with the Small Bath White, Eastern Dappled White and the female Orange-tip, but it differs in the following ways:

From Small Bath White
1. Underside of hindwing generally less streaked and with white discal patch circular rather than elongate.
2. Underside of hindwing with marginal white stripes

Bath White female

spanner-shaped rather than straight.
2. Upperside of forewing with white costal patch small and rounded rather than triangular or zig-zagged.
3. Upperside of forewing with white spots in dark marginal band not extending to the edge of the wing.

From Eastern Dappled White

1. Hindwing underside not irregularly blotched with white and pale yellow-green.
2. Hindwing underside lacking long, white, vertical median bar.
3. Forewing upperside with white apical patch smaller and more ovoid rather than rectangular.
4. Forewing upperside with white spots in dark marginal band not extending to the edge of the wing.

From female Orange-tip

1. Hindwing underside not irregularly dappled white and dark moss-green.
2. Forewing upperside with prominent white patches in the dark marginal band. See Figs 2&3 (p44).

Bath White male

SMALL BATH WHITE
Pontia chloridice (Hübner)

Small Bath White female. Matt Rowlings

Small Bath White male. Eddie John

Distribution and habitat
A rare and localised species found mainly in the Troodos region where it inhabits forest tracks, the margins of cultivated plots and rocky areas, such as dry riverbeds and disturbed ground where the larval foodplant grows.

Foodplant
The only known foodplant in Cyprus is the very localised Bird Spiderflower (*Cleome ornithopodioides*).

Flight period
Usually April to mid-October in

two or three generations.
Identification
Average wingspan 40mm.
Could be confused with Bath White, Eastern Dappled White and female Orange-tip but differs in the following ways:
From Bath White
See text for that species page 36.
From Eastern Dappled White
1. Underside of hindwing streaked rather than dappled.
2. Upperside of forewing with white apical patch linear or zig-zagged rather than square.
From female Orange-tip
1. Underside of hindwing streaked rather than dappled.
2. Upperside of forewing with bold, white, apical and marginal streaks.
See Figs 2&3 (p44).

Bird Spiderflower

Disturbed ground habitat near Kato Platres

LARGE WHITE
Pieris brassicae (Linn.)

Distribution and habitat
Very common and widely distributed throughout Cyprus in many habitat types.

Foodplant
Many species of mustard (Cruciferae).

Flight period
Throughout the year in four generations.

Large White female

Identification
Average wingspan 55mm. The markings are similar to those of the Small White, but the present species is much larger.

Large White male (England)

SMALL WHITE
Pieris rapae (Linn.)

Small White female

Distribution and habitat
Very common and widely distributed throughout Cyprus in many habitat types. It is often regarded as a pest in agricultural areas.
Foodplant
Many species of mustard (Cruciferae).

Flight period
Throughout the year in overlapping generations.
Identification
Average wingspan 40mm. The markings are similar to those of the Large White, but the present species is much smaller.

Small White male

EASTERN DAPPLED WHITE
Euchloe ausonia (Hübner)

Distribution and habitat
Common throughout most of Cyprus in many habitat types.
Foodplant
Several species of Brassicaceae, including White Mustard (*Sinapis alba*) and Shortpod Mustard (*Hirschfeldia incana*).
Flight period
Usually mid-February until early June in two generations.
Identification
Average wingspan 40mm. Could be confused with Bath White, Small Bath White and female Orange-tip but differs in the following ways:
From Bath White
See text for that species p36.
From Small Bath White
See text for that species p38.
From female Orange-tip
1. Underside of hindwing dappling yellow-green rather than dark moss-green.

Eastern Dappled White

2. Upperside of forewing with prominent white, square apical patch and conspicuous white marginal bars. See Figs 2&3 (p44).

ORANGE-TIP
Anthocharis cardamines (Linn.)

Distribution and habitat
Common and widespread throughout the south-western corner of the island but with a more localised distribution elsewhere. Prefers damp situations such as forest tracks and clearings, riversides and the edges of agricultural land where the foodplants flourish.

Foodplant
Several species of Brassicaceae.

Flight period
Mid-February to early May in a single generation.

Identification
Average wingspan 35mm. The male is unmistakeable. However, the female could be confused with Bath White, Small Bath White and Eastern Dappled White. See text pp 36, 38 & 42 for those species and Figs 2&3 (p44).

Orange-tip female

Orange-tip male

Fig 2 Hindwing undersides A Bath White, B Small Bath White, C Eastern Dappled White and D female Orange-tip.

Fig 3 Forewing uppersides A Bath White, B Small Bath White, C Eastern Dappled White and D female Orange-tip.

SMALL COPPER
Lycaena phlaeas (Linn.)

Distribution and habitat
Common and widespread throughout the island in many habitat types.

Foodplant
Several species of dock (*Rumex* spp).

Flight period
Usually from mid-February to late November in several generations.

Identification
Average wingspan 25mm. The only species with which this species might be confused is the Lesser Fiery Copper from which it differs in the following ways:

1. Much smaller than Lesser Fiery Copper.
2. Where present, the 'tails' of the hindwings are short. Those of the later generations of Lesser Fiery Copper are very long.
3. Hindwing upperside mainly solid black rather than orange with dark markings.
4. Hindwing underside lacking large, black spots and conspicuous orange band. See Fig 4 (p47).

Small Copper female

Small Copper male

LESSER FIERY COPPER
Lycaena thersamon (Esper)

Lesser Fiery Copper female

Lesser Fiery Copper male

Distribution and habitat
Widespread and common at lower elevations of the south-western half of Cyprus. It inhabits roadsides, scrubland and the edges of agricultural land, often in damper localities.

Foodplant
In Cyprus this species is restricted to Horsetail Knot-grass (*Polygonum equisetiforme*).

Flight period
Usually from mid-March to late November in up to four successive generations.

Identification Average wingspan 30mm. May be confused with Small Copper. See text for that species p45 and Fig 4.

Fig 4. Undersides of the coppers

Small Copper

Lesser Fiery Copper

LEVANTINE LEOPARD
Apharitis acamas (Klug)
subspecies *cypriaca* Riley

Levantine Leopard. Eddie John

Distribution and habitat
This endemic subspecies is scarce with a scattered and very localised distribution across the south-western half of the island. It can be found most frequently in scrubland interspersed with small bushes where the soil is dry and friable.

Foodplant
Unknown. The species appears to be highly associated with ants of the genus *Crematogaster* and the immature stages may be spent feeding on the ant's larvae in the underground brood chamber.

Typical habitat for Levantine Leopard with friable soil and sparse vegetation

Flight period
Late May to late October in at least two generations.
Identification
Average wingspan 30mm. This endemic subspecies always rests with its wings closed. In appearance it is unlike any other butterfly found in Cyprus.

PURPLE HAIRSTREAK
Favonius quercus (Linn.)

Purple Hairstreak female (England)

Purple Hairstreak male (England)

Distribution and habitat

Restricted almost exclusively to forested mountain districts centred on Paphos Forest and the Troodos region, where it is most common at higher elevations. Here it can be seen flying amongst the canopy close to, and around, its foodplant. It rarely comes to the ground but occasionally does so to drink from muddy puddles.

Foodplant

Golden Oak (*Quercus alnifolia*) and Aleppo Oak (*Q. infectoria*).

Flight Period

Usually late May to early September.

Identification

Average wingspan 35mm. The Purple Hairstreak is unlike any other species found in Cyprus.

Purple Hairstreak underside (England)

LANG'S SHORT-TAILED BLUE
Leptotes pirithous (Linn.)

Distribution and habitat
A locally common species in lowland areas where it inhabits forest clearings, scrubland, cultivated plots and gardens.

Foodplant
Polyphagous, including Lucerne (*Medicago sativa*), Camel Thorn Bush (*Alhagi graecorum*) and the ornamental garden plant Blue Plumbago (*Plumbago auriculata*) around which it may be seen flying in large numbers.

Flight period
Can be seen from March to December but most often recorded between June and October. There are several overlapping generations.

Lang's Short-tailed Blue female. Matt Rowlings

Identification

Average wingspan 25mm. May be confused with the other 'tailed' blues, Long-tailed Blue and Little Tiger Blue but differs in the following ways:

From Long-tailed Blue

See text for that species, p54.

From Little Tiger Blue

1. Underside markings not distinctly black-and-white.
2. Underside of hindwing with a pair of black-centered, irridescent blue spots at the base of the 'tails'.

See Fig 5 (p57).

Lang's Short-tailed Blue male

LONG-TAILED BLUE
Lampides boeticus (Linn.)

Long-tailed Blue female (Spain)

Distribution and habitat

An abundant and widespread species that can be found in many habitat types.

Foodplant

Many wild and cultivated species of the pea and bean family (Fabaceae).

Flight period

Usually from early March to late November but is occasionally seen during the winter.

Identification

Average wingspan 27mm. This is one of three species of 'tailed' blues found in Cyprus. It may be distinguished

Long-tailed Blue male

from the other two in the following ways:

From Lang's Short-tailed Blue

1. Forewings more pointed.
2. Underside markings linear and pale brown rather than with dark, grey-brown blotches.

From Little Tiger Blue

1. Underside markings linear and pale brown rather than distinctly black and white.
2. Underside of hindwings with a pair of black-centred, iridescent spots at base of 'tail'.

See Fig 5 (p57).

LITTLE TIGER BLUE
Tarucus balkanicus (Freyer)

Distribution and habitat
Fairly common along a broad lowland band approximately between Morfou Bay in the west and Larnaka Bay in the east. There are also small colonies around Paphos and Akrotiri Salt Lake. It is widespread in the central plains.

Foodplant
Restricted to Lotus Tree (*Zizypus lotus*).

Little Tiger Blue female

Little Tiger Blue habitat near Paphos

Lotus Tree (note the angular branches)

Flight period

Usually from late March to early November in several overlapping generations.

Little Tiger Blue male

Identification

Average wingspan 20mm. May be confused with the other 'tailed' blues, Long-tailed Blue and Lang's Short-tailed Blue. See the text for those species pp 52 & 54, and Fig 5.

Fig 5. Undersides of the 'tailed' blues

Long-tailed Blue   Lang's Short-tailed Blue   Little Tiger Blue

HOLLY BLUE
Celastrina argiolus (Linn.)

Distribution and habitat
Restricted to the south-western third of the island where it is found mainly in shaded localities, usually near water. Most often met within forested areas.

Foodplant
There are many recorded hostplants, most commonly flowers and buds of species of the pea family (Fabaceae).

Flight period
Usually early March to early October in three overlapping generations.

Identification
Average wingspan 27mm. The almost plain silver underside, with just a few tiny black dots, is unlike that of any other 'blue' butterfly found in Cyprus. See Fig 6 (p71).

Holly Blue female

Holly Blue male

EASTERN BATON BLUE
Pseudophilotes vicrama (Moore)

Distribution and habitat
A very localised species with a widely scattered distribution. It is most often encountered in lowland coastal localities or salt lakes. It inhabits scrubland where the larval foodplant thrives.

Foodplant
Restricted to Conehead Thyme (*Thymus capitatus*).

Flight period
Usually late February to early June in two generations.

Identification
Average wingspan 23mm. The distinctively black and white chequered forwing fringes and the silver undersides with bold, black spots are diagnostic of this species. See Fig 6 on p71.

Eastern Baton Blue female. Matt Rowlings

Eastern Baton Blue male

Conehead Thyme.

Typical habitat near Agios Georgios, Pegia

PAPHOS BLUE
Glaucopsyche paphos **Chapman**

Paphos Blue female

Paphos Blue male

Distribution and habitat
This endemic species is very common in the south-western half of the island and along the northern coastline. It occurs in many habitat types, including forests and scrubland where the larval foodplants thrive.

Foodplants
Several species of Broom (Fabaceae).

Flight Period
Usually from early February to mid-July in one or two generations.

Identification
Average wingspan 25mm. The very large black spots on the underside of the forewings are diagnostic. See Fig 6.

Typical habitat near Kathikas

DARK (AFRICAN) GRASS BLUE
Zizeeria karsandra (Moore)

Dark Grass Blue female. Matt Rowlings

Dark Grass Blue male

Distribution
Common in lowland areas, though apparently absent from the north-eastern quarter of the island. It can be found in many habitat types, including roadside verges, scrubland, cultivated plots and gardens. It prefers areas where the larval foodplant grows adjacent to bare earth.

Foodplants
Many low-growing plants, including Horse-tail Knotweed (*Polygonum equisetiforme*).

Flight period
Usually between March and October in overlapping generations, but can be seen throughout the year.

Identification
Average wingspan 20mm. The underside of the hindwing is rather plain pale brown with small, black dots and without the orange markings of similar species. See Fig 6 on page 71.

Typical trackside habitat near Kato Paphos

PERSIAN (SMALL) DESERT BLUE
Luthrodes galba (Ledera)

Persian Desert Blue female

Persian Desert Blue male

Distribution and habitat

An extremely localised species that inhabits roadsides, rough ground, pavements, walls and abandoned agricultural plots where its equally scarce foodplant grows. At present the butterfly may be found in such places around Lefkosia and the salt lakes of Larnaka and Akrotiri.

Foodplant

The sole foodplant is Mediterranean Mesquite (*Prosopis farcata*).

Flight period

Usually late May to late October in three overlapping generations.

Identification

Average wingspan 20mm. The pair of large, black spots partly surrounded by irridescent blue at the anal angle of the hindwing underside, along with the lack of orange markings, should preclude confusion with the other 'blues' found in Cyprus (see Fig 6, p71).

Mediterranean Mesquite growing amongst rubble on wasteground near Dromolaxia

GRASS JEWEL
Freyeria trochylus (Freyer)

Distribution
With the exception of the north-eastern peninsula and the extreme west of the island, this species is widespread, though very localised. It inhabits a wide variety of habitats, including rocky coasts, the edges of cultivated ground, roadsides and forest clearings.

Foodplant
Probably restricted to False Orpine (*Andrachne telephioides*).

Flight period
Usually from early March to early November in several generations.

Grass Jewel female. Matt Rowlings

Grass Jewel male

Identification

Average wingspan 15mm. This is the smallest butterfly in Europe. The uppersides of the sexes are similar. On the hindwing underside, the (usually four) large, orange patches containing irridescent blue-edged, black spots are diagnostic. See Fig 6 p71.

False Orpine

Rocky coast habitat near Kato Paphos

BROWN ARGUS
Aricia agestis ([Denis & Schiffermüller])

Brown Argus female

Brown Argus male

Distribution and habitat
Widespread in the southern half of the island and most often seen at higher elevations where it can be quite common. It inhabits forests and scrubland, often near water.

Foodplant
Not known in Cyprus, but the adults are often seen flying around *Geranium* and *Helianthemum* species.

Flight period
Usuall between mid-April and early October in several generations.

Identification
Average wingspan 25mm. Most easily confused with the female Common Blue, but the uppersides are completely lacking blue scales. Also, Fig 6 on page 71 shows the comparitive diagnostic patterns of black spots on the undersides of the hindwings.

Typical habitat near Agios Georgios, Pegia

COMMON BLUE
Polyommatus icarus (Rottemburg)

Distribution and habitat
Widespread and common in many habitat types throughout most of Cyprus.

Foodplant
Several species of the pea family (Fabaceae) and other low-growing herbs.

Flight period
Usually from late February to late November in several overlapping generations.

Identification
Average wingspan 30mm. The female is easily confused with Brown Argus. However, the uppersides of the present species always has at least some blue scaling. Also, Fig 6 opposite shows the comparitive patterns of black spotting on the undersides of the hindwings.

Common Blue female

Common Blue male

Fig 6. Undersides of the 'tail-less' blues A Holly Blue,
B Paphos Blue, C Dark Grass Blue, D Persian Desert Blue,
E Grass Jewel, F Eastern Baton Blue, G Brown Argus, H Common Blue

SOUTHERN WHITE ADMIRAL
Limenitis reducta Staudinger

Southern White Admiral upperside

Southern White Admiral underside

Distribution and habitat
Mainly a forest species that can also be found in tree-lined river valleys.
Foodplant
Restricted to Etruscan Honeysuckle (*Lonicera etrusca*).
Flight period
Usually late April to late September in three generations.
Identification
Average wingspan 50mm. The bold, white markings on the raven-black uppersides are unlike any other species found in Cyprus. The flight of this species is very elegant with long periods of gliding.

Typical habitat near Trooditissa

CARDINAL
Argynnis pandora (Denis & Schiffermüller)

Cardinal female upperside. Pieter Vantieghem

Cardinal male upperside

Distribution and habitat
Restricted to forested areas in the Troodos region.
Foodplant
Various species of violet (*Viola* spp).
Flight period
Usually from late May to late October but scarcely seen during the heat of Summer.
Identification
Average wingspan 70mm. This large, orange butterfly is unlike any other species found in Cyprus.

Cardinal underside

RED ADMIRAL
Vanessa atalanta (Linn.)

Distribution and habitat
A common species found in many habitat types throughout Cyprus.

Foodplant
Several species of nettle (*Urtica* spp).

Flight period
May be seen during any month of the year.

Identification
Average wingspan 55mm. Unlike any other species found in Cyprus.

Red Admiral upperside

Red Admiral underside (England)

PAINTED LADY
Vanessa cardui (Linn.)

Painted Lady upperside (England)

Painted Lady underside

Distribution and habitat
A very common butterfly that sometimes appears in enormous numbers. It can be found in all habitat types throughout the island.
Foodplants
Many and varied.
Flight period
Can be seen throughout the year.
Identification
Average wingspan 55mm. Unlike any other species found in Cyprus.

NETTLE-TREE BUTTERFLY
Libythea celtis (Laicharting)

Distribution and habitat
Very rare and localised. Found only in the forests of the Troodos region. It is now a legally protected species.

Foodplant
Restricted to European Nettle-tree (*Celtis tournefortii*).

Flight period
Usually between mid-April to late September. Hibernation is spent in the adult stage.

Identification
Average wingspan 37mm. The distinctive wing-shape and the extraordinarily long palpi or 'snout' preclude confusion with other species found in Cyprus.

Nettle-tree Butterfly upperside (France).
Gary Thoburn

Nettle-tree Butterfly underside (France).
Gary Thoburn

PLAIN TIGER
Danaus chrysippus (Linn.)

Plain Tiger. Steve Cale

Distribution and habitat

An occasional visitor to Cyprus during its spring and autumn migrations. Included here as it sometimes appears in large numbers and, following a large influx in 1998, several 'home-bred' individuals were noted but overwintering was unsuccessful. 2023 was also an exceptional year with local breeding taking place once more. The great majority of sightings have occurred at coastal locations.

Foodplant

Stranglevine (*Cynanchum acutum*).

Flight period

Usually seen during spring and autumn.

Identification

Unlike any other species found in Cyprus.

TWO-TAILED PASHA
Charaxes jasius (Linn.)

Distribution and habitat

A rare and enigmatic species of localised distribution. It is seen most often in forested areas where the larval foodplant grows. However, it has a great liking for over-ripe fruit and is a regular visitor to orchards and gardens where these occur near its breeding areas. It is also attracted to beer and this is sometimes used as 'bait' to attract the butterfly.

Foodplant

Mainly Eastern Strawberry-tree (*Arbutus andrachne*).

Two-tailed Pasha (France). Geoffrey Pring

Two-tailed Pasha (Mallorca). Jason Moss

Typical habitat near Pano Platres

Flight period
Two generations, usually from early May to early July and early August to the end of September.
Identification
Average wingspan 70mm. A large, powerful-flying and unmistakeable butterfly.

Eastern Strawberry-tree

LATTICE BROWN
Kirinia roxelana (Cramer)

Distribution
Widespread but uncommon in the south-western quarter of the island and along parts of the northern coastal hinterland. It inhabits shaded localities at higher altitudes such as river valleys, heavy scrub and dense hedgerows.

Foodplant
Various grasses.

Flight period
Usually from late April to mid-September.

Identification
Average wingspan 60mm. This large butterfly is unlike any other species found in Cyprus.

Lattice Brown. Dave & Ros. Sparrow

When disturbed, the Lattice Brown often flies into dense foliage and can then be difficult to find. David Cook

SPECKLED WOOD
Pararge aegeria (Linn.)

Speckled Wood female

Distribution and habitat
Widespread and locally common in the western half of the island where it usually inhabits wooded localities such as forest tracks and clearings and river valleys, often near water.

Foodplant
Various grasses.

Flight period
Usually from early March to late October in three generations, though may be seen throughout the year.

Identification
Average wingspan 40mm. This orange-spotted butterfly is unlike any other found in Cyprus.

Speckled Wood male

Typical semi-wooded habitat near Polis

LARGE WALL BROWN
Lasiommata maera (Linn.)

Distribution and habitat
Widespread and localised in the south-western half of the island and along the northern coastal hinterland. Here it favours rocky ground in forests, scrubland and the edges of agricultural plots.

Foodplant
Various grasses.

Flight period
Usually from early February to late October in at least two generations.

Large Wall Brown female

Identification
Easily confused with Wall Brown. See text opposite and Fig 7 a & b below.

Large Wall Brown male

Fig 7a. Undersides: Large Wall Brown,

WALL BROWN *Lasiommata megera* (Linn.)

Wall Brown female

Distribution and habitat
Widespread and locally common in the south-western half of the island where it inhabits rocky terrain along forest tracks and clearings, scrubland and the margins of agicultural plots. It is most frequently found at higher altitudes.

Foodplant
Various grasses.

Flight period
Usually from mid-February to late October in at least three generations.

Identification
Average wingspan 40mm. Easily confused with the Large Wall Brown. The uppersides of each species differ considerably, but the undersides are very similar. The present species differs from the Large Wall Brown in the following ways:

1. Underside of hindwing with submarginal line formed by an ornate series of semi-circles rather than a plain line.
2. Underside of hindwing with median line thicker and more indented.

See also Fig 7a on the left.

Wall Brown male

Fig 7b. Wall Brown

EASTERN ROCK GRAYLING
Hipparchia syriaca (Staudinger)
subspecies *cypriaca* (Staudinger)

Eastern Rock Grayling

Distribution and habitat
Mainly a forest-dwelling species of high ground such as that in the Troodos region. It is found throughout the south-western third of the island and also along the northern coastal hinterland. It sometimes visits orchards and gardens to feed on rotting fruit.

Foodplants
Various grasses.

Flight period
Usually from late May to mid-October.

Typical habitat near Pano Platres. The roadside trees and wall provide ideal perching places for this species.

BROWNS

Identification

Average wingspan 60mm. This endemic subspecies may be confused with Cyprus Grayling p88. The present species usually perches on tree trunks or walls rather than on the ground. It always rests with its wings closed. The ground colour of the underside of the forewing is pale brown in this species and orange in Cyprus Grayling. The underside of the hindwings lacks the sharply angled and indented median band seen in Cyprus Grayling. In flight this species appears very dark by comparison with Cyprus Grayling.

CYPRUS GRAYLING
Hipparchia cypriensis (Holik)

Cyprus Grayling

Cyprus Grayling in typical resting pose with forewings hidden

Typical rocky coastal habitat near Kato Paphos

Distribution and habitat

This endemic species is widespread and common in suitable habitats throughout most of Cyprus. It can be seen in forests, scrubland, rocky ground and coastal localities.

Foodplant

Various grasses.

Flight period

Usually mid-April to late October.

Identification

This species may easily be confused with Eastern Rock Grayling. See text for that species (p86).

THE HERMIT
Chazara briseis (Linn.) subspecies *larnacarna* (Oberthür)

Distribution and habitat
Widely distributed and common in many habitat types throughout most of Cyprus.

Foodplant
Various grasses.

Flight period
Usually from late April to mid-October.

Identification
Average wingspan 60mm. This large, black and pale-cream butterfly is unlike any other species found in Cyprus. It always settles with the wings closed.

The Hermit

BROWNS

The Hermit resting with forewings hidden

Typical flowery habitat near Agios Georgios, Pegia

WHITE-BANDED GRAYLING
Pseudochazara anthelea (Hübner)

White-banded Grayling female

White-banded Grayling male

Distribution and habitat
Found at higher altitudes, mainly in and around the Troodos region but also around Keryneia in the north. It inhabits forests and scrubland where it can be seen in rocky areas and along wooded tracks, clearings and roadsides.

Foodplant
Various grasses.

Flight period
Usually from late April to late September.

Identification
Average wingspan 50mm. Always settles with its wings closed. The bold, white band on the hindwing of the male makes it unmistakeable. The female hindwing is very plain by comparison with the other grayling species. The pair of white spots between the two ocelli on the underside of the forewing is diagnostic.

White-banded Grayling female showing the diagnostic white spots on the forewing underside.

AFRICAN RINGLET
Ypthima asterope (Klug)

Distribution and habitat
Very scarce and localised. Found mainly in the lowlands of western and central-northern Cyprus. It inhabits rocky scrubland and dry riverbeds.

Foodplant
Various grasses.

Flight period
Usually from early March to early June and again from early September to late October.

Identification
Average wingspan 33mm. The very large eye-spots on the upperside and underside of the forewings preclude confusion with other species.

Typical upland rocky habitat

BROWNS

African Ringlet

African Ringlet showing large forwing eye-spots

CYPRUS MEADOW BROWN
Maniola cypricola (Graves)

Cyprus Meadow Brown female

Distribution and habitat
A very common endemic species found throughout Cyprus in many habitat types.
Foodplant
Various grasses.
Flight period
Usually late April to mid-October.
Identification
Average wingspan 45mm. This endemic species can easily be confused with the Oriental Meadow Brown (see p98) but differs from that species in the following ways:
1. Male upperside of forewing with conspicuous orange flush rather than completely very dark brown.

Cyprus Meadow Brown male

2. Female upperside of forewing with bright orange patch rather than dark brown with two conspicuous eye-spots.
3. Male underside of hindwing usually with at least one small but bright yellow-ringed eye-spot. These are absent in Oriental Meadow Brown.
4. Male underside of forewing more extensively orange with dark marginal band narrower and encircling less of the eye-spot.
5. Female underside of hindwing with very striking markings rather than being plain.
6. Hindwing edges less scalloped.
See also Fig 8 (p99).

ORIENTAL MEADOW BROWN
Hyponephele lupina (Costa)
subspecies *cypriaca* Riley

Oriental Meadow Brown female. David Cook

Oriental Meadow Brown male

Distribution and habitat
A common species that is widely distributed in the western half of the island. Here it is most often found on higher ground, including that of the Troodos range. It inhabits forest tracks and clearings, scrubland and the edges of agricultural plots.

Foodplant
Various grasses.

Flight period
Usually early May to late September.

Identification
Average wingspan 45mm. The male uppersides of this endemic subspecies are often indistinguishable from those of the Cyprus Meadow Brown. See text for that species (p96).

However, the pair of large, black spots on the upper- and underside of the female's forewings are diagnostic of the present species.

Fig 8. Undersides of Cyprus Meadow Brown and Oriental Meadow Brown. A Male forewing underside, B Male hindwing underside, C Female hindwing underside

Cyprus Meadow · Oriental Meadow

Index of Species

acamas, Aphartis 14, **48**
acteon, Thymelicus 13, **28**
Admiral, Red 15, **76**
Admiral, Southern White 15, **72**
aegeria, Pararge 15
African Migrant 16
agestis, Aricia 14, **68**
alceae, Carcharodus 13, **30**
anthelea, Pseudochazara 16, **92**
Anthocharis 14, 43
Aphartis 14, 48
Aporia 13, 35
argiolus, Celastrina 14, **58**
Argus, Brown 14, **68**, 70-1
Argynnis 15, 74
Aricia 14, 68
asterope, Ypthima 16, **94**
atalanta, Vanessa 15, **76**
aurota, Belenois 16
ausonia, Euchloe 14, **42**
Azanus 16

balkanicus, Tarucus 14, **56**
Belenois 16
Blue, African Babul 16
Blue, African Grass 14, **62**
Blue, Common 14, 69, **70**, 71
Blue, Dark Grass 8, **62**, 71
Blue, Eastern Baton 14, **59**, 71
Blue, Holly 14, **58**, 71
Blue, Lang's Short-tailed 14, **52**, 55, 57
Blue, Little Tiger 14, 53, 55, **56**, 57
Blue, Long-tailed 14, 53, **54**, **57**
Blue, Paphos 8, 11, 14, **60**, 71
Blue, Persian Desert 14, **64**, 71
Blue, Small Desert 14, **64**
boeticus, Lampides 14, **54**
brassicae, Pieris 13, **40**
briseis, Chazara 16, **90**
Brown, Lattice 15, **82**
Butterfly, Nettle-tree 11, 15, **78**

Carcharodus 13, 30
cardamines, Anthocharis 14, **43**
Cardinal 15, **74**
cardui, Vanessa 15, 77
Catopsilia 16
Celastrina 14, **58**
celtis, Libythea 15, **78**
cerisyi, Zerynthia 13, **22**
Charaxes 15. 80
Chazara 16, 90
chloridice, Pontia 13, **38**

INDEX OF SPECIES

chrysippus, Danaus 15, **79**
Cleopatra 13, **32**
cleopatra, Gonepteryx 13, **32**
Colias 13, 34
Copper, Lesser Fiery 14, 45, **46**, 47
Copper, Small 14, **45**, 47
crataegi, Aporia 13, **35**
croceus, Colias 13, **34**
cypriaca, Aphartis acamas ssp 14, **48**
cypriaca, Hipparchia syriaca spp 15, **86**
cypriaca, Hyponephele lupina ssp 16, **98**
cypricola, Maniola 16, **96**
cypriensis, Hipparchia 15, **88**

Danaus 15, 79
daplidice, Pontia 13, **36**
Deudorix 16
demoleus, Papilio 13, **20**

Euchloe 14, 42

Favonius 14, 50
Festoon, Eastern 11, 13, **22**
florella, Catopsilia 16
Freyeria 14, 66
Fritillary, Queen of Spain 16

galba, Luthrodes 14, **64**
Gegenes 13, 26
Glaucopsyche 14, 60
Gonepteryx 13, 32
Grayling, Cyprus 11, 15, 87, **88**
Grayling, Eastern Rock 11, 15, **86**, 89
Grayling, Great Steppe 16
Grayling, White-banded 16, **92**

Hairstreak, Pomegranate 16
Hairstreak, Purple 14, **50**
Hermit, The 11, **90**
Hipparchia 15, 86, 88
Hypolimnus 16
Hyponephele 16, 98

icarus, Polyommatus 14, **70**
Issoria 16

jasius, Charaxes 15, **80**
jesous, Azanus 16
Jewel, Grass 14, **66**

karsandra, Zizeeria 14, **62**
Kirinia 15, 82

Lady, Painted 15, 77
Lampides 14, 54
Lasiommata 15, 84, 85
lathonia, Issoria 16

INDEX OF SPECIES

Leopard, Levantine 11, 14, **48**
Leptotes 14, 52
Libythea 15, 78
Limenitis 15, 72
livia, Deudorix 16
lupina, Hyponophele 16, **98**
Lycaena 14, 45, 46

machaon, Papilio 15, **18**
maera, Lasiommata 15, **84**
Maniola 16, 96
Meadow Brown, Cyprus 11, 16, **96**, 98, 99
Meadow Brown, Oriental 11, 16, 97, **98**, 99
megera, Lasiommata 15, **85**
misippus, Hypolimnus 16
misippus, Papilio p…

Nymphalis 16

Orange-tip 14, 36-9, 42, **43**, 44

pandora, Argynnis 15, **74**
paphos, Glaucopsyche 14, **60**
Papilio 13, 18, 20
Pararge 15, 83
Pasha, Two-tailed 15, **80**
Pelopidas 13, 24
persephone, Chazara 16
phlaeas, Lycaena 14, **45**
Pieris 13, 40, 41

pirithous, Leptotes 14, **52**
polychloros, Nymphalis 16
Polyommatus 14, 70
Pontia 13, 36, 38
Pseudochazara 16, 92
Pseudophilotes 14, 59
pumilio, Gegenes 13, **26**

quercus, Favonius 14, **50**

rapae, Pieris 13, **41**
reducta, Limenitis 15, **72**
Ringlet, African 16, **94**
roxelana, Kirinia 15, **82**

Skipper, Lulworth 13, **28**
Skipper, Mallow 6, 13, **30**
Skipper, Millet 13, **24**, 26, 27
Skipper, Pigmy 13, 25, **26**, 27
Speckled Wood 15, **83**
Swallowtail 13, **18**
Swallowtail, Lime 11, 13, **20**
syriaca, Hipparchia 15, **86**
syriacus, Papilio machaon ssp 13, **18**

Tarucus 14, 56
taurica, Gonepteryx cleopatra ssp 13
thersamon, Lycaena 14, **46**
thrax, Pelopidas 13, **24**
Thymelicus 13, **28**

Tiger, False Plain   16
Tiger, Plain   11, 15, **79**
Tortoiseshell, Large   16
trochylus, Freyeria   14, **66**

Vanessa   15, 76, 77
vicrama, Pseudophilotes   14, **59**

Wall Brown, Large   15, **84**, 85
Wall Brown   15, **85**, 84
White, Bath   13, **36**, 38-9, 42-4
White, Black-veined   13, **35**
White, Brown-veined   16
White, Caper   16
White, Eastern Dappled   14, 36-9, **42**, 43-4
White, Large   13, **40**, 41
White, Small   13, 40, **41**
White, Small Bath   13, 36-7, **38**, 42, 44

Yellow, Clouded   13, **34**
Ypthima   16, 94

Zerynthia   13, 22
Zizeeria   14, 62

Checklist

1. Swallowtail *Papilio machaon*
2. Lime Swallowtail *Papilio demoleus*
3. Eastern Festoon *Zerynthia cerisyi*
4. Millet Skipper *Pelopidas thrax*
5. Pigmy Skipper *Gegenes pumilio*
6. Lulworth Skipper *Thymelicus acteon*
7. Mallow Skipper *Carcharodus alceae*
8. Cleopatra *Gonepteryx cleopatra*
9. Clouded Yellow *Colias crocea*
10. Black-veined White *Aporia crataegi*
11. Bath White *Pontia daplidice*
12. Small Bath White *Pontia chloridice*
13. Large White *Pieris brassicae*
14. Small White *Pieris rapae*
15. Eastern Dappled White *Euchloe ausonia*
16. Orange-tip *Anthocharis cardamines*
17. Small Copper *Lycaena phlaeas*
18. Lesser Fiery Copper *Lycaena thersamon*
19. Levantine Leopard *Apharitis acamas*
20. Purple Hairstreak *Favonius quercus*
21. Lang's Short-tailed Blue *Leptotes pirithous*
22. Long-tailed Blue *Lampides boeticus*
23. Holly Blue *Celastrina argiolus*
24. Little Tiger Blue *Tarucus balkanicus*
25. Eastern Baton Blue *Pseudophilotes vicrama*
26. Paphos Blue *Glaucopsyche paphos*
27. Dark Grass Blue *Zizeeria karsandra*
28. Persian Desert Blue *Luthrodes galba*
29. Grass Jewel *Freyeria trochylus*
30. Brown Argus *Aricia agestis*
31. Common Blue *Polyommatus icarus*
32. Southern White Admiral *Limenitis reducta*
33. Cardinal *Argynnis pandora*

CHECKLIST

34 Red Admiral *Vanessa atalanta*
35 Painted Lady *Vanessa cardui*
36 Nettle-tree Butterfly *Libythea celtis*
37 Plain Tiger *Danaus chrysippus*
38 Two-tailed Pasha *Charaxes jasius*
39 Lattice Brown *Kirinia roxelana*
40 Speckled Wood *Pararge aegeria*
41 Large Wall Brown *Lasiommata maera*
42 Wall Brown *Lasiommata megera*
43 Eastern Rock Grayling *Hipparchia syriaca*
44 Cyprus Grayling *Hipparchia cypriensis*
45 The Hermit *Chazara briseis*
46 White-banded Grayling *Pseudochazara anthelea*
47 African Ringlet *Ypthima asterope*
48 Cyprus Meadow Brown *Maniola cypricola*
49 Oriental Meadow Brown *Hyponephele lupina*

Notes

NOTES

Notes

NOTES

More Books by Brambleby Books

A Weed-Lover's Calendar:
Secrets of those errant plants revealed
Rachel Fulcher
ISBN 978-1908241740

Discovering British Wild Flowers
Deirdre Shirreffs
ISBN 978-1908241634

An Invertebrate Fable –
Ten Sequences of poetry about insects, gastropods & arthropods
Simon Zonenblick
ISBN 978-1908241696

Bee Tiger -
The Death's Head Hawk-Moth through the Looking-glass
Philip Howse
ISBN 978-1908241627

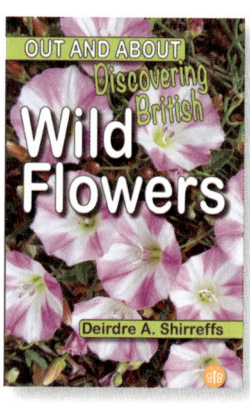

www.bramblebybooks.co.uk

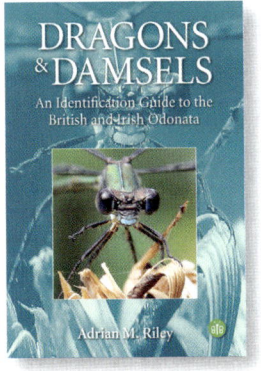

The Butterfly Collection –
A poem for every British butterfly
Richard Harrington
ISBN 978-1908241566

Dragons and Damsels –
An identification guide to the British and Irish Odonata
Adrian M. Riley
ISBN 978-1908241641

British and Irish Butterflies
– The complete Identification, Field and Site Guide to the Species, Subspecies and Forms
Adrian M. Riley
ISBN 978-0955392801

MORE BOOKS BY BRAMBLEBY BOOKS